Pierced by the Seasons
Living a Life on the Coast of Maine

Poems and Haiku
Elizabeth W. Garber

Elizabeth Garber

For mom,
For the woman who has no
time to ~~read~~ read! I
hope this book of poems from
our good friend helps t
slow you down and get,
you through the winter !
2004
#2
sm

The Illuminated Sea Press

2004

"First of September, Belfast, Maine" was previously printed in *Meridians*

Printed in Maine

ISBN 1-9761311-0-2

The Illuminated Sea Press
66 Miller St.
Belfast, Maine 04915

Dedicated to

My children Gabriel Photeos and Miriam Sophia
My dear friend and colleague Vicki Cohn Pollard
And to my mother, Jo Garber, who has always encouraged me

Contents

What it Takes to Get Through the Winter in Maine

What It Takes to Get Through the Winter in Maine

We probably wouldn't choose it, staying here all winter,
if we weren't so rooted in like the indigo mussel shells
grasping onto the ledges as the daily tides of winter
wrap and batter and wear us smooth.

The winter is a series of heartaches and reprieves.

It begins with the first cold days that crash in so fast
the last week of August, like a slap to the side of the face,
leaving us bereft, grieving the softly warm luminous days.
Suddenly sobered, we are left facing
what it will take
to get through the winter.

That summer, so sweet, so short, the blue washed light
over the shimmering sea, the blissful handful of days
the waves were warm enough to enter.
Skin alive and radiant, sun filled, granite sparkles illuminating eyes
shining over campfires on evenings that stretch out so long.
Those days when some tender place in us relaxes and trusts
that we are held and supported in this warmth,
as the sea holds us so buoyantly.

Then the spell is broken.
The first cold warning softens soon enough,
but nothing is the same again.
We feel older, wearied, humbled.
This is what winter brings us,
again and again,
tide after tide,
wearing away at us,
teaching us to surrender
to the darkness, the cold, the fear.

Now is the time to gather up what we need
for getting through the winter, and
I don't mean getting the wood in and the house banked,
the windows sealed, the doors muffled.

The winter is a series of heartaches and reprieves,
and each one hits harder than the last,
shearing us as bare as the trees.

We need to stock the root cellar
with enough Ball jars of canned ripe peaches
to open the remembrance of sunlight into dark winter days.
We need to stock up enough captivating books to draw us
expectantly under our deep covers for the long cold night.
We need to know enough warm kitchens we can step into
where arms will embrace us
and warm voices will rise to surround us.
We need to engage in enough good work that will grasp us strongly
and work us hard and well on days we can't bear another storm.
We need enough music so songs will rise up out of our bellies
and take us singing out into the long icy drive home.
We need enough points of contact so that our hold
in the storm will be enough to make it through.

Winter's work is to take us to our greatest fears,
to break us down, and work us hard.
We have to strengthen that muscle
that anchors us to the rock of the winter sea,
holding us steady.

We don't know if we will be enough to make it through the winter.

This may seem like a warning,
but really, it's winter's challenge,
an invitation.

First of September,
Belfast, Maine:
Late Summer into Fall

First of September, Belfast, Maine

awakened, startled by the enormous stillness
the great golden hymn of August gone quiet
the first chill touch of bare feet on floorboards
as wide as the forests of 1850

slipping out the screen door
past deserted streets of white clapboard houses
the white edged windows wide eyed,
the gardens weary, the hostas tired,
the arch of day lilies flagging

the morning light faded, like a favorite shirt
left forgotten on the clothesline all summer,
washed out blue-gray light of bay and horizon
as I slide into the chill of the harbor, paddling out

miles of sea morning moving through my arms,
my back, my mind:
the milling urgent fascinating voices of summer
washing out of my mind
the great brilliant momentum of heat and color
washing out of my mind
the last kiss of that lush abundance called August
washing out of my mind
slipping out with each slice and slide of paddle
into still salt sea
slipping ever quieter until I reach
the stillness of the cormorants

those jet black silhouettes of elegant curving necks and beaks
lining the ordered layers of granite of the monument
guarding the bay
silent dark candles on an ancient cake
all facing northeast,
all utterly still, completely quiet,
a quiet of a shared bird mind,
standing for eons under this sky
hurtling over their stillness

when I open my eyes again,
they are far behind me,
the rising morning wind gently
sending me back towards shore
where the first sailboats slip south
slicing through the faded light

September Full Moon Haiku

river in moonlight
paddling in black and white
following your voice

How to Position Oneself in Regards to the Leaf of Happiness

Children have been told
that if you catch the autumn leaf
before it hits the ground
you will receive a month of happiness.

They hurtle themselves, leaping
into the air, stretching out to reach and grab it
before they collapse giggling into
that great mound of rustling happiness.

My friend, when walking beside the sea,
saw a tree sigh like a mother sinking
into a chair after her last child has left home.
"That tree let down all her leaves in 20 minutes," he said.
"I caught about 3 years of happiness.
And here." He gave me one of the leaves.

This morning after the first early snow,
I walk along examining the leaves remaining on trees,
wondering how long I would have to wait for that solitary aspen leaf
wavering like a loose tooth ready to give way?

I pass the great oaks fully clothed in their rich brown leaves
knowing they will not relinquish their grip until the last snow
  of winter.
I pass the rare tree still glistening in reds and greens
and know it is too vibrant to let go of
any of its happiness.

Then I pass under a branch and look up,
to see a tiny almond-shaped, golden leaf and a single seed pod,
luminous against the pearly gray-blue sky.
And that solitary still life gives me
all the happiness I need.

An Afternoon of Stories

What can be more marvelous than an afternoon of stories?
Those stories arriving unbeckoned,
flooding up as if surprised to find themselves
leaping forward with such enthusiasm,
chasing after each other, as eager as
the wondrous dog who studied birds so carefully
that she folded her legs back like wings and leapt into flight.
Those stories as insistent as the silky cat who steadily makes his way
to be snuggled in under the chin, body stretched over the storyteller's chest,
eyes adoring the face where stories keep emerging.

Stories appear in the pauses,
they bubble up in times of waiting,
around tables in lamplight, while waiting for late night buses,
waiting for blizzards to pass, for babies to be born.
These are the spaces outside of time,
when stories can take us by surprise.
Each place becomes marvelous.
The velvety night sky, blue couch becomes a stage,
the stools at the counter become a Hopper painting.
The lamplight warms the edges of the storyteller's face,
the background disappearing into Rembrandt-rich shadows.

Meals can wait,
cats can hurtle themselves against the side of the house
clamoring to come in, calls to be returned can blink their red lights,
and chores can always wait when there is a story to be told.
The house opens its cavernous ears, and says, "Hush, be still,"
and the chimes that persistently give voice to the northwest wind go silent.
All are waiting for the stories.

Like collections of jeweled necklaces,
stories arrive, hand knotted together,
like a line of fishes all caught with the same bait.
Collections of stories, to be held up to the light,
the next popping in so fast to catch the tail of the last,
with pauses for chuckles, "Oh yeah's,"
the rise and fall of nodding heads, the tiny pause, space, ponder
and then the next story can't wait another moment.
It may usher in a new collection.
Some are gaudy costume jewels of feisty stories;

some heavy weighted, well-polished precious gems
of stories of beloveds;
some stories are collections of gallstones
gathered in a cup after surgery, hard and prickly,
grown from years of irritations;
some stories are ephemeral,
strung together snowflakes of such beauty
and never repeated patterns, which vanish in their one brief telling;
and some are rare pearls still wet from the deep salt sea of grief.

And the ones, who sit back outside the lamplight,
who lean forward to receive these stories,
whose breath quickens and calms with the rise and fall of stories,
whose quiet laughter and catching of eyes
and smiles of recognitions encourage the stories,
but never enough so that it breaks the stream.
The listening ones lie back, resting,
as they are fed the food of stories,
savoring the combinations of flavors,
twirling the succulent tastes and textures around their mouths,
taking in the scents of stories as the wine connoisseur swirls the glass,
  wondering what course will be next,
and is this dessert?

Until the spell breaks,
and time returns. The snowplow etches the world with sound.
The way is cleared. The wind whips sound back into the chimes.
It is time to leave the circle of light, to leave into the dark storm,
for the baby to be born, the cats to be fed, the children put to bed.
It is time for the stories to return
to their great hand-carved chest under the stairs
to gather for that next calling,
that next pause between worlds,
waiting for those who walk between heaven and hell
to call out to them saying,
"Yes, we are waiting for you."

Kayaking Back to Stonington Harbor
Before the Early November Dark

gray-white light ripples
reflected in evening
riding water home

The Gift

On my birthday, I dream twice of being
a seal woman alive at the surface
of the ocean, in my embodied life.
Wide-eyed delight watching the world
of granite islands, water and sky,
and when I dive down
the cold water flows
across my eyes as I swim.

My silky strong seal body.
flowing muscles,
moving, part of the water.
Wide eyed awake and watching.
I am as open to the enormous light sky
as I am to the enormous dark water.
Playing at the surface,
choosing whether to go up to the light
or down into the dark.
I have no preference.
Fearless, completely at ease,
going into either realm.

Steering Clear

I can get so lost
in a sweet falling asleep,
in a dance of such fluidity,
adapting so gently, so easily
to whomever I am needed to be,
lulled into forgetting so easily,
as I give myself away in kindness
to everyone else.

I have to grab myself awake,
splashing myself alive with cold salt spray
laughing myself out loud in great wide expanses
of light and eyes wide open watching life alive
remembering where I am enough of me,
enough of who I truly am
so that I do not forget myself

in that utterly effortless turning,
again and again to become the one
the other has always wanted.

I will keep turning my bow into the wind
feeling the edges of my true self
up against the edge of granite
and sweep of sea.

This sea that has come so far
to hear me laugh in delight
to be riding its great swells.

Remembering,
remembering this is who I am,

just delight over water
in a moment of November dusk light.

The House of Grief

You can't go into the House of Grief
and think you will leave untouched.

Even when we offer ourselves as a gift,
as a balm for another's pain,
Grief takes us into her embrace
and with a wave of trembling
we are taken into the forgotten place
of our own ancient tears.

Instructions for Caring About a Widower

To care about a widower means
to hear the story of love from one
who has gone to the gates of hell
and has been sent home alone.

To care about him means
to return with him to the places
he has scattered her ashes,
to the mountain where he let the winds take her,
to her favorite islands where the water received her.

   (He is telling you,
    "This is how I loved")

To care about him means
hearing the story etched in his mind
of those last wearied days when
he passed beyond enduring
standing sentry at the doorway
helplessly as she slipped past him.

   (Listen, he is letting you know,
    "This is how I loved")

To care about him means
we cannot know, but we can gather into our heart
how terrible was the labor of his returning to this life.

Do not ask why her photos are still around the house.
Do not ask why haven't you let go of her jewelry.
Do not ask have you gotten over this yet.

Do not ask stupid questions!
The only place to stand is in awe.

We are being given a gift we do not know.

Hungry for a Poem

I leave the heated scurry of cooks,
the rising tides of related voices,
the pack of little cousins tearing through the kitchen,
and walk the dusk path to the ocean,
hungry for a poem.

Poems cannot be summoned
like relatives confirmed to arrive for the feast
with the favorite cornbread sausage stuffing,
or the cranberry apple walnut compote,
or the apricot linzertorte.

Poems will gather their own ingredients, stolen
from scraps of conversations,
from the last dream tangle at dawn,
from the wild bramble before the dunes begin,
from the pale green light that blossoms in the sea
as the sun pierces the November surf for just a moment.

Poems come in their own time,
savoring the currents of sounds,
the wafting textures of consonants,
the snarl of choice words to tease the tongue.
Their recipe so resistant to discovery,
they could hold up dinner for days,
so poems are taken off the menu.

Long after the families have scattered
back across the map.
After the long journeys home in the dark
over ferries and inland winding ways,

that elusive poem arrives with the dawn light
in the happiness of my own pillows,
and the words falling into rhythms in my mind
bring a satisfying sweetness that
feeds a hunger no feast ever touches.

Love arrives in Winter, Smiling

Eight Degree Morning in Belfast Harbor

sea smoke swirling out
crossing the bay of brilliance
warm in purring car

On Meeting at King Eider's Pub Where the Christmas Tree Is Decorated with Oyster Shells

toasting with oysters
bright cold swallow with lemon
later your soft lips

That Terrible Weight

There is a terrible weight that can settle in
over Christmas and leave it so saddened.
This siege of wanting
that squeezes out any joy.
A wanting no gift can ever fill,
an expectation no surprise can ever lift.

Can you feel it? There in your chest,
that heaviness that leaves the eyes weary.
And the mind, that sad old accountant,
adding up the evidence, that no gift can ever balance out.
See, the voice says, affirming with a strange glee,
see, they never gave me what I wanted.
See, they never knew me.

And yet something can happen.
You could wake up at 2 a.m. on Christmas morning and
feel a simple happiness to be warm in your covers.
You could find the day weightless and simple.
You could look around, in slow motion, in wonder,
and it could feel so simply light, so simply a day.
You could watch your children open presents
and see they are content with what is simply enough.
You could realize in that moment
you don't need anyone to give you anything,
and when someone hands you a package
you could feel a gentle pleasure in being surprised.

And when the great swirl of snow begins,
layering the world in great drifting seas,
your 72 year old mother could give you
the best gift ever, to invite you all out to play.
You could bundle up against that stinging wind and
make snow angels and run into each other, laughing.
You could all venture down the dark path into the woods
singing "Lions and tigers and bears, oh my"
and your mother could sneak up behind you and
say, "Watch out for monkeys!"
and you could realize this is the first time
you remember that she's played with you
since you were a little girl.

And later, you could climb into those freezing guest beds
with your almost teenaged daughter and you could both
shriek and squeal, "Oooohhh, cold cold cold,"
as your toes stretch into those icy sheets,
and you could laugh so much,
and your daughter could stretch her arms around you
so happy to be playing like a kid with her mom,
and sleep with her arms around you all night.

And you could suddenly see
that pearl that has been floating down
across the time of your entire life,
dropping toward your outstretched palm
all this time,
and you could receive such joy.

Winter Short Stories

1.
On walking out into the Christmas blizzardy Night

black velvet seal dogs
wrestling by, in the snow waves
crashing around us

2.
On awakening at 5 a.m. with lines in my head
in a house full of extended family

smile between two worlds
life when a poem is cooking
a secret pleasure

3.
On returning home to climb through 3 feet of drifted
snow to reach the basement stairs to find the snow shovel

happily sleeping
two old gray watering cans
and red snow shovel

4.
On returning home and realizing
there is a long winter ahead

drawing in lamplight
five pears in a yellow bowl
food for a winter

5.
On returning to the paths at Tanglewood

skiing white velvet
through silent white pine forest
in radiant dusk

6.
On taking my favorite long summer walk along
the Belfast tide line in late December

razor's edge between
drifted snow and ice rivers
low tide sandy steps

7.
On letting out the cat this January morning at 5:30 a.m.

bite of cold on feet
iced blue snow at dawn light
cat returns quickly

8.
On skiing down to Ducktrap River after the second blizzard
of January

thick muscled water
pouring past ice-capped boulders
fills hemlocks with sound

Love Arrives in Winter, Smiling

your poems arrive
from silent gray glowing screen
leaving me breathless

you open my door
receiving my eyes smiling
love enters beaming

dangerous cold night
love catches me by surprise
and fear vanishes

sharp biting walk home
warming in your arms all day
quiet between words

the lamp at my bed
warming the scent of our love
holding you all night

watching dawn arrive
your face appearing slowly
dark eyes grow hazel

(after you've left)

too awake to sleep
the cat purring at my feet
4 a.m. haiku

Breathing You into Me

I awake in the dark.
The sound in every breath is your name.
Every part of me is suffused with your voice,
your laugh, your speaking,
all touching me.

Every object I pass as I put out the cat
into the deep blue dawn is your name
before it is the lamp, the chair, the door.
The air in every breath is filled with you.

We are breathing each other into ourselves.

I know I am Elizabeth, but your name interweaves me.

7 a.m. Belfast Harbor at 20 below

sea smoke tidal wave
drowning my town in ice fur
moon silvered sun disc

Carrying You with Me while I Snowshoe Alone

snow-filled deep forest
gray-green lichen lace on birch
your eyes smiling through

essential quiet
stream freezes over to rest
can you hear nothing?

traveling lightly
snowshoeing through spruce wood
carrying haiku home

the joy of your voice
fills the blue lit meadow
saturated smile

dusk shimmers golden
in the branches of white pine
where do I begin?

coming home to warmth
filled with cooking and laughter
I will see you soon

Living in the Quiet House of Winter

snow settles on roof
my love finds a place to rest
deep winter sleeping

longing's tide recedes
the desperate search for love
vanished with your touch

at home in your eyes
smiling inside of blizzards
at our feet, dog sleeps

Winter Terrors

It's a terrifying thing to open a heart
so crushingly wide open
so fast
terrifying to risk so much
"I couldn't ever do this again"
we both knew
thought we knew

trying to create safety
certainty, a container to hold back our fear,
yet we opened wide the jaws of fear
as we dove in
trying to stay awake
as we fell into each other's mouths
tasting the swirl of the river lilies

not knowing we'd committed ourselves to swimming underwater
until we scared ourselves out of breath

Spring's Dangers

Spring's Dangers

at winter's breaking
a precarious balance
forget to trust spring

agonizing wait
risking, risking, missing you
crushingly cold spring

my house misses you
the man who swims in my bed
reaching out to me

March Sap Rising: on the first long walk
after weeks of arctic winds driving us all inside

hope soars with sunlight
soil sealed in ice 5 feet deep
willows glow yellow

salt sea meets the ice
smell of seaweed and mussels
refreshing kisses

beach draped in ice quilt
stepping very carefully
first walk in sneakers

Ode to Sebastian

I'm lying in bed, luxuriating in poems at ll:15 in the morning
on a day of commerce in the world beyond.
How wild to abandon all the calls to vacuum and errand
to lie in bed reading poetry
to lie in bed, my body yearning for your touch.

The gaining light of mid-February is moving the roots
in the great line of maples out my window.
Those roots living deep in the ground, under
the solid sea of iced winter and frost aching earth.
Yet even under the great seal of ice,
the roots are moving.

I can tell. I saw the spark in my cousin Kate's 68-year-old eyes
as she told me of finding that old knowing, that finding her way
on dear safe old Sebastian's saddled back
as she rode in the stable for the first time in 30 years.
"You know," she said, "it was just like getting into bed
with an old lover," and her eyes leapt with Spring's arrival
as she leaned back her head and laughed with such warmth
that we knew the back of winter had been broken.

On sitting beside Damariscotta Lake on a mild March morning, gazing out over the vast expanse of water sheathed in ice 2 feet thick

a slow gentleness
ice remembering water
surrendering form

Skunk Cabbage Dreams

The only thing moving this raw April dusk
on this still island miles off the Maine coast
are the silent dark legions of skunk cabbage
arising from every mossy wet hummock.

These ancient tangles of swollen architecture,
twisted python hooded deep purples,
erupting green streaked silken dancers,
each standing open mouthed to a different darkness.

Their cousins, primordial age-stained stone nagas,
hooded snake spirits worshiped from the earliest times,
cluster at the roots of ancient tree temples in South India,
erupting out of the same ancient earth mind

What emerged first is unknown to us now,
disturbing, discomforting, speaking a primordial language,
their roots snaking down into our forgotten reptilian rivers of mind,
when we each stood open mouthed to our own darknesses.

Leaving the pierced darkened marshes,
I go back to the tiny haven of light.
We eat long-simmered soup made from roots,
celeriac, yellow beets, leeks, onions, garlic,
and we sleep, sinking deeply into our dreams,
surrounded by the silent, open-mouthed marshes.

In the Changing Rooms
(For my 14 year old daughter)

I think it was when we both bought "glam shine" lip gloss
and sat in the car in the raw light of an April parking lot,
laughing so hard that we could hardly
stroke on this buttery glittery cream of outrageousness,
that we knew this was a different kind of day,
as Mimi called it, a "totally girly day."

A rare day, rising out of the tidal familiarity of a winter
of waking in the dark, waiting for the shower, breakfast bagels,
rides to school, and evenings of homework and struggles,
sharing the computer for both of our umbilical desires to connect.
A winter spiced with comments of my toughest critic,
who was sure I was going out of my way to annoy her, regularly;
drawing attention to my sighs of frustration,
saying, "Oh, no! Not your 'Oh, I'm so deep' voice."

I'm the kind of mom who has the same tube of lipstick
I had when my daughter was born, saved for those rare moments
an ex-hippie, sensible mother remembers to add a splash of color
to liven up Maine small town life, and where shopping is another
rarely remembered activity.
But today, with lips glinting, we head into the forest of aisles,
searching for sensible comfortable clothes for summer.

In the changing rooms, under fluorescent skies, naked to the mirrors,
the interior review of our bodies begins again.
Stepping into the old movie
I began as a girl with my mother crowding into one snug space,
as we searched through clothes trying to find who we were,
and watching the other's body to know who we weren't.
So many years of harsh reviews of thighs and breasts and now,
I am surprised by my kindness toward living in my well-worn skin.

I watch my daughter, shoulders strong and upright,
wearing her vibrant body without fear,
no sinking inward, no hiding,
no incesting hand grasping at her blossoming.
I protected myself with my wit and sensible clothes.
She wears her clothes in delight with her womanliness.

As a teenager, I felt I brought my mother up, teaching her to dress.
Now I watch my daughter determined to do the same.
"How can you wear those old lady pants?
Un-tuck your shirt! It looks so stupid!"

We both put our faces in that strange "looking in the mirror look"
  of concentration
as we walk back and forth, trying out what seems needed, necessary,
  and cool.
But as we search for the next skin to try out,
selves we've never known
start to talk to us through the language of fabrics.

We lose all sense of time,
We hover, at a cusp of leaving, and then another voice steps in,
I say, " Mimi, I know this is crazy,
 but I want to go back and look at something again."
I have to try on a life I've never lived.
There is this slinky red silk suit and short skirt that started talking to me,
and a pair of sexy little black heels that I couldn't walk five steps in,
but I have to try them on.
Mimi gathers up an armful of long slinky dresses,
and we head back for the changing rooms.

We stand in front of that three-way mirror,
trying on possible futures.
We each twirl, and examine ourselves, and laugh.
Who is this woman up here so high on shoes so precarious?
But my legs never looked like this in Birkenstocks!
Who is this young woman sashaying in her evening dress?

We exchange, trying on each other's fantasies.
My daughter who just the week before had pronounced
with absolute clarity while doing homework,
"I could be a senator, couldn't I, Mom?"
And now standing there in that silk suit,
I see the girl who could be senator.
I try on her silky twirling layers of soft greens and rose
and see a summer's evening garden party
lit with luminarias and blues piano.
And I have to find pretty sexy little shoes to go with it,
shoes I may only take five steps in,
but I have to take those slinky steps never taken.

And Mimi keeps laughing, "Mother, I need to restrain you!"

The Fear of Poetry

In the lists of ever more exotic, and specialized fears,
way beyond the familiar fear of heights, fear of dark nights,
fear of crowds, and fear of falling, beyond all that,
there is the fear of poetry.

I watch for the subtle eye-widening glance of fear,
before the blocking and pushing away with the casual aside,
"I never was one for poetry."

The fear ingrained from the eyebrow-raised teacher
unfurling in your direction the question,
"What is the significance of that phrase in the poem considering
the time and circumstances of when it was written?"
And your mind went blank.

Or the deep discomfort when the excited friend,
exuberant on words that touch her,
wants you to be moved,
but the words when you read them
are an unopened gate.

Oh, why can't we sink into the words,
and let them rise around us
as if I were diving down through the layers
in that great warm bog, Hurd's Pond,
sliding past the red-green leaves of the wild cranberry and
the open pitcher plants, vases catching rain and black flies.

I keep diving through the mat of mosses and pale lichens,
the maze of entwined roots of this floating island,
descending into the life of the bog,

My slippery body hurtling downward in slow motion,
my hair rising up like stems of the water lilies grasping for the surface,
my nostrils wide open to breathe in this well-seeped,
dark tea of ancient pond life.
Sliding down through the gauze-fine layers of seasons,
soil memories of a winter long and snowy like this one,
and a spring like that one.

If only poetry would rise to receive us like that bog.

If only we could all be so comingled,
then the poems would seep into our veins,
and there would be no separation
and no fear.

Requiem (for a cocoon of love)

I called out to you
I sang to you across the waters
My voice filtering down in the pause between the waves,
drifting, settling, slipping deeper,
following the silvered threads of light
that sew through the depths
deep into the coracles of your deep swimming ears

you received my voice
and a listening began,
a listening so steady, so ferocious, so merged
that our listening bodies became one
ear to ear, mouth to mouth, eye to eye

two bodies sleeping into each other cell to cell
falling into a sleep of utter completeness
turning to rise and fall entwined like waves traveling great distances
    together,
ocean crossing waves entangled water to water,
breath to breath,
hairs to hairs
breathing as if one, turning as if one,
entangled breast within breast,
in a warmed sea cocoon

where the joy was beyond knowing
the laughter beyond beauty
the sweetness beyond tasting

in a land outside time,
in a land untouched by air and wind and fine scuttled clouds
or maybe it was a land that was only air and wind and such fine clouds
in a land that disappeared between breaths
in a land turning transparent in the sunlight
in a land disappearing by the minute
in a land beyond land, under a wave beyond wave,
in a touch, breathed full of touch
in a whisper breathed full of silver threads
in a current beneath all currents
our voices tumbled
in the glistening sand washed salted billowing,

breathing through the smell of the sea,
our voices listening, breathing, sleeping into each other

yet some joinings cannot be held up to the sun to be seen,
and that grasping to become solid
begins to break the gossamer threads

some ripplings of light are only seen for a moment
some minglings are known only a fraction of a second
in the time of the world

I called to you and your solitary tender presence opened
knowing at the moment of opening that this was the last opening,
dying from the beginning
beginning as a dying
the dying was born the moment the call was answered

the work is to live beyond dying
to curl up and sleep in the warm arms of this blessing
this blessing of awakening again
awakening to be fed by the tangled seas of words
awakening again and again,
to listen to the currents within currents of songs
to find laughter again and again
in the belly of the world, in the warm belly of the sea

in the warm toes on the beach of the heart
the brilliant glowing sand,
the glistening sand made from the shattered sea-scoured shells,
those shells that once met in their eternal embrace
now sea worn, sea wrestled, sea softened,
sun warmed, this brilliant glowing sand
fills this cove, sun filled and lit within,
holding these feet as if they are the first steps ever taken

In My Little Town
this Week: Summer

On Walking to Belfast Harbor Summer Mornings at 6 a.m.

every morning
past houses to the hill crest
there you are, shining

Venus Crosses the Sun

warm scent of lilacs
snuggling into my hair
summer's first kisses

In My Little Town This Week

Following my 8 a.m. quiet morning walk to work,
down Miller past the old brick Crosby school,
along Church Street, passing the upright First Church and brick
  Court House,
springing with each step since I've already walked two miles along the
  ocean.

Looking forward to a day of patient stories,
from the comfort of my 20th year of listening.
Smiling, I take the granite steps at the familiar corner
looking ahead to the Victorian triangular treasure of a building,
which graces the center of town.
When suddenly I see in the corner window,
a golden sculptured dance of forms, arching over
the palest dawn of light.
In that moment I think, it's the jewel in the crown,
blessing us.

At my office, the stories of lives and pain and healing
rise up around me, as I swim through their currents,
like swimming this first warm week in July
in Knight's Pond, sliding through the warm and cool layers
while damsel flies circle and dance and scatter across the surface.
The threads of stories tying so many of our lives together,
criss-crossing like smiles across the street, and in the grocery store.
We have known each other so long.
And then in midstream, a story pierces through.
A friend's husband, just my age,
a great wounded powerful stag of a man,
has dropped to his knees and died,
the night before.

I find myself watching everything more closely, lingering a little
  longer, in each moment.
The silhouette of the lobsterman standing in his boat heading out in
  the deep fog at 6 a.m.
The woman in her eighties standing watching the bay, telling me that
  she's always taken her first swim on May 31st, yet it's been too cold
  this year. Today she thinks is the day for her first swim.
And when the fog breaks and the blue sky appears, strangers stop on
  the street to admire the sunlight, talking like old friends.

Each moment standing out in relief, with space to pause, to notice a little more carefully.

Time slows down as my friend tells me every moment of these last days. How he watched her drive away. "He stood there lingering so long, that last morning. It was almost weird. I kept watching him staying there watching me like he'd never done before. And all day as I worked I watched the house of a woman whose husband and son had died within two months, and I'd said out loud, it must have been six times, "How could you ever survive that?"

There is such stillness, like not breathing for a long time, sitting with friends pierced by death. She wrote in his obituary today, "He was a man gouged by many griefs." His best friend, a woodworker said, "In wood, gouges are just in the surface. His were much deeper than that."

So this is how this story ends. I can't believe I'll never hear his voice again. I just wanted a little more time. I just wish I could go too.

He's already appearing in the dreams of friends, telling funny stories. "I know I'm dead, but I left this video of me so it could be played in real time." Telling another with his voice clearly in his ear, "I'm so relieved to be out of that body." That weighed down battered heavy body. It is hard work to live in this body.

And I leave her side and walk slowly, dream like,
up Main street, up the steep long staircase, to exercise,
in a room where sunlight pours through the white curtains.
My breath feels so quiet. I can only move very quietly,
slowly, and time spreads out with a vastness around me.
I watch my toenails glimmer like mother of pearl.
I feel my lifting up out of my ribs to arch over my leg,
all in slow motion, paying attention to all of it.
A car drives by in the street below
and the voice of James Taylor drifts in
sweetly with an old song of comfort.
And we smile with such fondness,
for all of this.

For all of this.

Feasting

I am so amazed to find myself kissing you
with such abandon,
filling myself with our kisses
astounding hunger for edges of lips and tongue.
Returning to feast again and again,
our bellies never overfilling from this banquet.
Returning in surprise,
in remembering,
in rediscovering,
such play of flavors of gliding lips
and forests of pressures and spaces.
The spaces between the branches
as delicious as finding the grove of lilies of the valley
blossoming just outside my door under the ancient oak.
"I've never held anyone this long," you said,
the second time you entered my kitchen.
I am the feast this kitchen was blessed to prepare
waiting for you to enter open mouthed in awe
in the mystery we've been given,
our holy feast.

This Man Whose Sacred Landscape Is Women

His whole life he has made of himself an offering,
kneeling down, leaning forward, offering his tongue
to the hidden petals of heat nestled in fur,
learning to speak in tongues and touch
devoting himself to discovering this lost language of generosity.
There are so many ways to bow down in prayer.

His story is the chronology of women loved.
He wears their stories, layers of antique kimonos,
layers and layers of fine worn silks,
silk skins of scents that float and trace
his finely carved longing.
They are all a part of him and he wears them well.

Krishna, the blue skinned god, hints his presence
at the shadowy edges of his eyes,
in the dissolving iridescent magic of his lips.
Krishna and his consorts dance their passion forever,
each one loved within their own eternity

Don't lose yourself in your own jealousy mazes
when he tells you of his loves.
He is telling you his treasury of a life of study,
of journeys taken, grails searched for,
a pilgrimage to temples of devotion, anointing
each one with the red vermilion powder.

He reads the sacred braille texts of our bodies
with the tips of his golden lion paws.
He drinks the smells of woman,
savoring the moistened muscled curves,
connoisseur of resistance disappearing into pleasure,
discerning artist unlocking thresholds of sighs.

His kohl-edged gaze will turn you sultry beyond imagining,
his glancing tongue will glisten your fur with golden flames,
the twirling lilting flavors of his voice will tickle your delight,
and when you draw down the silken veil of his honeyed sweetness
you will receive the smoky bite of mystery.

Who knows how long it is your destiny to linger in this temple
simply allow yourself to be the feast
simply allow yourself to be fed.

Summer Quintet

1.

Still waiting for summer.
It's the end of July.
A patient told me the last
visible sunrise she noted in her journal
was July 7th. It's been fog
every morning since.

This misty morning as I cross the street
at what was once the only stoplight in Waldo County,
I meet my feisty friend Eunice.
Early 70's, her sight receding, a widow
keeping her family business going,
she greets me with such certainty,
and conspiratorial glee.
'We are so fortunate to live here.
 The fog really doesn't matter."

2.

All the joy in the world
  can be found in sweeping this old pine floor.
All the joy in the world
  can be found weeding this small garden.
All the joy in the world
  can be found in smiling at one old friend.

Just let the happiness saturate you,
like the warmth rising out of this lush summer meadow
as the fog draws upward and vanishes into light.

3.

After weeks of thick green-gray light muting all of us,
when the moon pours through
we have to go out canoeing into this astounding clarity.

It's after 1 a.m., when
we pull alongside the tiny island on Toddy Pond.
We climb over the scramble of granite boulders,
to the clearing in the middle, just big enough for our blanket.
We lie down, three in a row, like cousins at a sleep-over,
applauding the stars shooting through the tall masts of pines above us,
the loons calling, the night getting darker as the moon sets.
In this time outside of time,
remembering,
this is summer.

4.

It takes courage to go swimming in the ocean here,
even on the first of August at the favorite secret beach
where the tide comes in a long way over the sun-warmed mussel beds.

But I like exercising courage.

Standing in the water, waist deep, getting ready to
go the next steps deeper, I think about
when I bundle up for my five-block walk to work,
when it's 30 below zero.
My breath icing into the scarf over my face,
only my stinging eyes showing.
My first patient and I go stomping up the stairs,
our laughter so lively and warm.
It's great to feel you've done something courageous
just walking to work,
and it's only 8 o'clock in the morning.
What's next?

5.

The cat rolls on his back in his sleep
in the garden, his paws floating in the air,
the sun on his furry tummy.
The nasturtiums cascade mounds
of red and yellow and orange blossoms.
The tomatoes are growing out of bounds.
The squashes look like something in a rain forest.

All the weeding is done for this year.
I can't remember that urgent planting fury
that grabbed me this spring, creating these new gardens.

We are now in the pause before the harvest.

Quiet happiness,
swinging on the porch swing,
moving it with just the push of one foot.
My daughter's long legs stretched over my lap.
Not wanting to move
or do anything,
except this.

A Summer's Garden Party

There are days that become little legends in the history of a summer.
Signposts. Each of us placing ourselves where we were
the night the moon came out after weeks of rain,
when the misty meadows were lit with fireflies
tracing streams of light.
There was the day the double rainbows dipped into the ocean,
and the day in town when people heard music
coming out of the trees,
and they went searching for it.

The piano was on my back deck, graced with lilies.
Our friends dressed in summer's elegance, and
Mary Anne's hands were liquid silver over the keys.
When she sang an aria from the Marriage of Figaro,
her arms extended out, sewing through the branches
into the calm, cloud-scalloped sky of early evening.

One woman remembered shouting "Bravo!" at La Scala,
and the men remembered the woman they'd always loved.

I Gave You Stories and Gardens:
A Song for My Son on His 18th Birthday

I gave you stories and gardens
and traveling quietly together.
We'd drive over the long hills home,
you in your car seat next to me.
I'd hold your sturdy little hand
as we'd watch the light change together,
pointing out the clouds branching so high above us.
We still drive, watching.
Your long young man's body in the driver's seat
hurtling us over these same hills,
as the etched shadows of clouds
pour over the wooded hills below us.

Stories read aloud
were the pillars of your days.
The morning beginning with "Read, Mommy, read,"
as you'd climb into our bed with your new pile of books.
The nights ending with either your Dad or me, lying beside you,
often falling asleep before you as we read aloud.
You had your elbow ready,
to butt us awake to read,
just a little more.

We traveled listening to stories.
Riveted by Odysseus in the Cyclops's cave,
you sat in the car in the school parking lot
until he'd escaped, holding onto the ram's thick wooly underbelly.
Traveling a long journey with The Lord of the Rings,
their language becoming ours in the dark,
in the heartbreak of Mordor,
we'd turn to look at each other,
tears in our eyes when their grief pierced our own.

I gave you gardens.
Everywhere I live, gardens emerge out of the landscape.
Pregnant with you, I planted
apple trees and poppies beside the Marsh Stream in Brooks.
When you were four, we began new gardens together.
We called the roots dragons as we wrestled
each wily tail out from the old rock wall,
creating new gardens next to the meadow high on the hill.
When you were nine, you discovered the joys of tree pruning.
We'd stand back to look
before we choose which next branch to cut
to shape the star magnolia.
Now, you examine my new gardens in town near the sea,
letting me know what you think I need to prune.

I gave you stories and gardens
and your father.
So many children keep drifting back into their mother's field,
and I kept steadily returning you
to the arms of your noble father.
He gave you your jet-black thatch of hair,
already hinting white, and
your deep Greek eyes, surveying our lives.
He carried you snuggled against his chest
the day you were born,
taking you into his shop over the stream.
Introducing you to the clean smell of freshly planed poplar,
ready to become the strong rails of ladders,
to stretch up into the branches of apple trees.
He said, "This is my world."
He gave you your long sinewy body,
the language of strong hands and tools,
an eye for the grain of wood,
a nimble mind to solve any challenge,
the goodness of hard work,
the generosity of his heart,
and the playfulness that tickles you both into laughter.

I gave you stories and gardens,
and you gave us our life,
that we created for you.

Visitations

There are moments, scattered across our lives,
when the thought hits us,
yes, we are alone.

Eighteen years ago today,
in the last thirty-six hours of childbirth,
when that moment came, it was a shattering,
a free fall into an aloneness, vast and endless,

and yet broken apart,
I was given my son
as my gift of opening to love.

Today, the moment came like a sigh,
a soft release of breath,
and I dropped into that sigh, unresisting,
Yes, this is my life. This is my aloneness.

And around me rose the singing of late summer,
the vibrant song of cicadas in the grass,
and the song seemed to be in everything,
in every breath of air I moved through.
It rose like comfort around me,
the wild tangle of Queen Anne's lace along the road felt like comfort
and the first yellowed leaves scattering felt like comfort.

After walking through the early heat of the day rising across the sea,
I stepped into the shadow of the great arching maple,
and felt the comfort of trees,
of coolness,
of shelter,
and wonder for this vast rising of limbs above me.

I fell into astonishment under that tree,
alive in the wash of gentleness,
in the currents of sounds
and breezes.

An Invitation

Make of your kitchen a hearth
 where you warm and nourish your life.

Make of the sky over your town your temple
 where you refresh yourself daily.

Make of the people in your town your Beloved
 to rediscover with kindness each day.

Make of the earth of your town your own garden
 where you gaze with attention each day.

Make of your life a steady flame of delight.

Look around you in this moment and see
 how all of this, pierces us with pain and such happiness.

About the Author:

Elizabeth W. Garber was born in 1953 and grew up in a village in Ohio. She has lived on a square-rigged sailing ship, and on a dairy farm in France. She studied mythology and Greek epic at Johns Hopkins and Harvard, worked as a renovation carpenter in California, and received her Masters in Traditional Five Element Acupuncture and has been practicing this for 20 years in Belfast, Maine.

Her previous collections of poetry are *Finding the Beloved: A Personal Journey to Recover the Divine from Centuries of Devastation* (1991), created along with painted sculptures and performed with a chorus of singers 12 times in New England over two years, including at the University of Maine at Orono and at Harvard Divinity School; *Grabbing Down Deep into the Wailing Room and Re-Emerging Through the Fire* (1993) performed with drummers and a slide show of photographs; *The Salmon Man's Bride* (1993); *At the Moment of Meeting: All Can Be Known* (1994) a series of poems written in collaboration with the artists Robert Shetterly and Louise Bourne for a show of paintings, sculptures, and poetry exploring the themes of the Annunciation at the Frick Gallery in Belfast, Maine. These collections were published in limited editions.

Acknowledgements

I am deeply grateful for my friends who have encouraged my writing for years, especially Kate Barnes, Louise Bourne, Diane Brott Courant, Squidge Davis, Martha Derbyshire, Stephen Huyler, Rick Jaeckel, Alexandra Merrill, Kate NaDeau, Vicki Cohn Pollard, Deborah Rose, Michelle Walker, and my Acupuncture colleagues.

I am grateful for those who have inspired these poems, for my family's steady loving presence, for Peter Baldwin and our thoughtful co-parenting of our wonderful children, for my patients who teach me so much, and for my community that nurtures living a creative life.

I am so grateful for the creative collaboration with Gretchen Warsen's enthusiasm and graphic design, Louise Bourne's generous sharing of paintings, Elizabeth IlgenFritz's invaluable copy editing, and Ray Estabrooke's printing expertise that brought this book into form.